Co-Create Your

Abundant,

Passionate

Purposeful Life!

If found, please return to:

Name:

_____

Phone:

_____

 Heart's Joy

www.hearts-joy.com

Cover designed by Elise Rorick, Lusicovi Creative.
Cover Artwork by Elise Rorick and JoHenna Design.
Henna Art designed by JoHenna Design.

ISBN: 9781096586067

Hey Magical Musing!

Congratulations on purchasing your new best friend! This journal is designed to empower you to co-create your life every day for the next 3 months!

Here's some insight into my morning routine and how I use this journal. I give thanks when I wake up; sit in my meditation area where I begin with chanting for 5 minutes and then continue for 10+ minutes of silent meditation; and then I stretch. I focus the next 15+ minutes on journaling using this daily journal! If you miss one day, that's okay — each day is a new start. This journal sets you up for a successful day giving you action steps in alignment with what your Angels are communicating with you, how you desire to feel, and your intentions!

The next few pages will show you how to create the desired feelings and intentions you'll focus on over the next 3 months. If you'd like help creating your desired feelings and/or intentions go to https://hearts-joy.com/daily-journal-how-to/

I'd like to thank JoHenna Design for creating the gorgeous artwork throughout the journal! Tap into your creative side as you color each Spirit animal. Check out her website at JoHennaDesign.com for art and henna.

Your future-self thanks you for taking time and showing up.

Sending you Much Love!
Karmen

How to Use the Journal

We are constantly co-creating every day with the energies in the Universe, with your Angel Guides, and with God. Everything and everyone is energy and this is how we're connected, through invisible energetic cords. This journal guides you to co-create your abundant, passionate purposeful life in partnership with God!

I believe that God is energy and that energy lives within each of us, also called your inner-Divine-self. This is the energetic cord that connects each of us. We all desire to be Loved, to be seen, to be heard! If the word God doesn't resonate with you, replace it with a word that resonates.

This journal offers both a morning and nightly focus. There's power behind having a morning and an evening practice. In the morning, you're co-creating your day and setting yourself up for a successful day! In the evening, you're again co-creating and setting yourself up for a successful morning.

After you learn about each journal prompt, start where it resonates with you. Let's vtake a walk through each journal prompt.

Morning Prompts

Step 1:
Create your desired feelings for the next 3 months. Desired feelings are guideposts of what you desire to bring into being!

Knowing how you'd like to feel brings clarity to creating your intentions and your daily actions. How we feel dictates everything else and how you'll show up each day! You're empowering yourself each day to co-create your daily experience.

"What you seek is seeking you." — Rumi

Before you create your desired feelings, take a look at each life area.
* Finances
* Career & Passion!
* Romantic Relationships
* Lifestyle (possessions, fashion, home, travel)
* Health & Wellness
* Inner-Divine-Self & Spirituality
* Creativity, Learning, Growth
* Family & Society

Page 1

Keep your *THOUGHTS* positive
because your thoughts become your words.
Keep your *WORDS* positive
because your words become your behavior.
Keep your *BEHAVIOR* positive
because your behavior becomes your habits.
Keep your *HABITS* positive
because your habits become your values.
Keep your *VALUES* positive
because your values become your destiny.
                              –Mahatma Gandhi–

These are the areas you'll focus on as you create your desired feelings. Let's get started!

First answer these questions in each life area (listed above) to clarify and claim your desired feelings:
1. What do I appreciate and why?
2. What's not working and how is that impacting me?
3. What I would like to do, experience, and have?
You'll notice some overlapping in each area. Go through and choose 3-6 desired feelings. Once you choose them, go over them again and notice if they have similar meanings, for example, joyful and playful. Ask yourself, will feeling playful lead to feeling joyful? Next choose your final 3-6 desired feelings for the next 3 months!

Desired feelings for the next 3 months:

_____

_____

_____

For each day in your journal, you'll choose 3 of these as a focus. For the monthly portion of your journal, you'll write individual intentions for each life area.

Step 2:
It's time to create your intention for the next 3 months using your desired feelings!

Intentions definition (noun)
1. an act or instance of determining mentally upon some action or result.
2. the end or object intended; purpose.

Intentions set the tone for what you anticipate experiencing in the life you're co-creating! As you create your intention, grab 1-2 of the main desired feelings to start your intention, "I intend to experience _____ and _____ as I _____." Then after "as I _____" these are what you intend to call into your life! For example, my intention is: "I intend to experience freedom and clarity as I empower people to joyfully connect with their inner-self and learn to live on purpose and in Divine Harmony."

You're choosing this intention for the next 3 months embodying your inner-Divine-self and co-creating with God! This intention is a bigger picture, a larger goal you desire to accomplish. This will be the same each day in your journal.

My intention for the next 3 months:

_____

_____

Step 3:
Your Daily Intention is focused on what emotion you intend to create that day.

For example: I intend to create inspiration and Love today! I intend to create harmony and peace today.

Step 4:
Next it's time to create I AM statements!
"I AM" are the two most powerful words! Whatever comes after "I AM" comes to fruition! Example, I AM tired or I feel tired. When you say I AM, you start to BE tired.

Your words are prayers co-creating with God. Remember we're all energy connected through these energetic threads and this includes our words we say. By the way, the Universe doesn't know when we're joking or being sarcastic!

Each day you'll create I AM statements (3-5). This allows you to focus on co-creating you day and standing in your power. If at first you aren't feeling it, write down one of these to get you started: I AM powerful. I AM creative. I AM co-creating. I AM empowered. I AM Love. I AM aware. I AM fun. I AM wise.

Step 5:
Affirmations vs Mantras

Affirmations are statements to help rewire thought patterns towards a more desired outcome.

Mantras are words or sounds either in Sanskrit or another language that allow you to focus on deepening your meditation while connecting you with God. Some people use them while they chant too.

Each day you'll choose 3-5 affirmations and/or mantras to focus on that day!

Step 6:
It's action time! Each day write 1-3 new action steps today you'll take to co-create your intentions! This doesn't have to be a large action step. In fact, baby steps will get you there quicker because it's not as overwhelming as a larger action step. Sometimes a larger action step is too much for us and we end up procrastinating and not doing anything. Baby steps! Feel free to place a check mark next to it after you complete it. Notice how each journal prompt builds upon the other. The only one that doesn't change until after 3 months is your intentions.

Step 7:
Today's Permission Slip!
What are you giving yourself permission to do today that you typically are hard on yourself? Some examples: have fun while working, take time to eat, take breaks every 2 hours, and move my body every 2 hours.

Evening Prompts:
Step 1: What are 3-5 appreciations from today and why?

Appreciation vs. Gratitude

Appreciation is more action-oriented and truly co-creating or calling-in more of what you desire. Gratitude says thank you yet there's still a form of lack as you didn't have it before and now you do.

Be sure to write down why you're appreciative as this reaffirms with the energies and will continue to call in more! Also feel free to write down what you appreciate in advance as another way to co-create!

During this time, really FEEL it in your body as if it's happened. The feeling is again another energy sent out co-creating. Your body doesn't know the difference if you already have it or not.

Step 2:
What are 3 qualities you love or value about yourself?

These are different daily and can include: I love my laugh, I value my persistence, I love my smile, I love my body, I value my meditation practice.

Step 3:
How do you desire to feel before bed?

Why ask this? Well, you're co-creating with the energies in the Universe, with your Angel Guides, and with God. One way your Angels communicate with you is in your dreams.

Step 4:
Questions for you Angels before bed.

This goes hand in hand with the last question. Since your Angels are communicating with you in your dreams, I'll ask them what they would like me to know and to show this to me in my dreams. Even if I don't remember it, my subconscious mind did. Another invitation is for me to experience a restful sleep and wake up feeling refreshed!

If you don't already, start to write down your dreams and feel free to use this journal! Each morning as soon as you awake, write down your dreams then give appreciation for a new day, new beginning, and new opportunities!

Monthly:
Each month there are prompts allowing you to check-in and re-adjust if needed.

Step 1: *Numerology*
Understanding our "numbers" through numerology, shows us our Soul Contract. Our Soul Contract is a contract of lessons our Soul chose before we came to Earth. As we understand our Life Path, our Challenges/Lessons, our Personal Year, and the monthly energies we can use this information when we make important decisions in our life. For example, the numbers help you know when the energies support you to launch a project or when the energies support you during change. For our purpose in this journal, the focus is to understand your Personal Year, and Personal Month. So let's get started!

Your Personal Year goes from your birthday in your current year to your birthday the following year, cycling a Personal Year 1 through a Personal Year 9, and then beginning the cycle once more. How to calculate your Personal Year:

Take Your Birth Month + Your Birth Date + Current Year = Personal Year (MM/DD/YYYY)

Example (March 3, 2020):

$3 + 3 + 2 + 0 + 2 + 0 = 10 = 1 + 0 = 1$ Personal Year

Always continue to add and get to a single digit.

The energies from your current Personal Year begin to shift 52 days before your birthday to the next Personal Year.

Your Personal Month is the energies of each month of the Personal Year you are currently experiencing. How to calculate your personal month:

Take your Personal Year that you calculated above + the number of the specific month in question = Personal Month

Example:
   1 (Personal Year per above) + January (1) = 2 Personal Month
   1 (Personal Year per above) + February (2) = 3 Personal Month
   1 (Personal Year per above) + March (3) = 4 Personal Month

Always continue to add and get to a single digit.

To understand what each number means as a Personal Year and a Personal Month, visit www.hearts-joy.com. Let's dive-in to the rest of the monthly check-in!

Step 2: You'll write down all your desired feelings for 3 months and notice if they still resonate.

Step 3: Next you'll write down your intentions for 3 months in every life area!

Step 4: Ask yourself, who do you need to be to manifest these intentions? How will you show up to co-create these intentions?

Step 5 & 6: Evaluate what's not working and why as well as what is working and why! This shows you where to implement any changes.

Step 7: Are my actions in alignment with my values? You'll list your values and write down how your actions are in alignment with your values in each life area listed.

Monthly

Check-In!

Month _____ **Year** _____
Personal Year _____ **Personal Month** _____

You'll write down all your desired feelings...

_____

_____

_____

Next you'll write down your intentions in the areas you're focusing on...

_____

_____

_____

_____

_____

Who I get to be to manifest these intentions

_____

_____

_____

What's not working & why?

_____

_____

_____

What's working & why?

_____

_____

_____

Are my actions in alignment with my values?

My values:

_____

_____

Life Areas

Inner-Divine-Self & Spirituality

Romantic Relationships

Family & Society

Health & Wellness

Lifestyle

Career & Passion!

Financial

Creativity, Learning, Growth

Co-Create

Daily Focus

Day _____ **Date** _____

How would I like to feel today? (choose 3)

_____

_____

My intention for the next 3 months

_____

_____

_____

_____

My daily intention

_____

_____

I AM (3-5)

_____

_____

Affirmations or Mantras

_____

_____

_____

1-3 action steps I can take today to co-create my intentions!

_____

_____

_____

_____

_____

Today's Permission Slip

_____

_____

Evening!

3-5 Appreciations from today and why

_____

_____

_____

3 Qualities I Love and value about myself

_____

_____

_____

How I'd like to feel before bed

_____

_____

Questions for my Angels before bed

_____

_____

_____

Day _____ **Date** _____

How would I like to feel today? (choose 3)

_____

_____

My intention for the next 3 months

_____

_____

_____

_____

My daily intention

_____

_____

I AM (3-5)

_____

_____

Affirmations or Mantras

_____

_____

_____

1-3 action steps I can take today to co-create my intentions!

_____

_____

_____

_____

_____

Today's Permission Slip

_____

_____

Evening!

3-5 Appreciations from today and why

_____

_____

_____

3 Qualities I Love and value about myself

_____

_____

_____

How I'd like to feel before bed

_____

_____

Questions for my Angels before bed

_____

_____

_____

Day _____ **Date** _____

How would I like to feel today? (choose 3)

_____

_____

My intention for the next 3 months

_____

_____

_____

_____

My daily intention

_____

_____

I AM (3-5)

_____

_____

Affirmations or Mantras

_____

_____

_____

1-3 action steps I can take today to co-create my intentions!

_____

_____

_____

_____

_____

Today's Permission Slip

_____

_____

Evening!

3-5 Appreciations from today and why

_____

_____

_____

3 Qualities I Love and value about myself

_____

_____

_____

How I'd like to feel before bed

_____

_____

Questions for my Angels before bed

_____

_____

_____

Day _____ **Date** _____

How would I like to feel today? (choose 3)

_____

_____

My intention for the next 3 months

_____

_____

_____

_____

My daily intention

_____

_____

I AM (3-5)

_____

_____

Affirmations or Mantras

_____

_____

_____

1-3 action steps I can take today to co-create my intentions!

_____

_____

_____

_____

_____

Today's Permission Slip

_____

_____

Evening!

3-5 Appreciations from today and why

_____

_____

_____

3 Qualities I Love and value about myself

_____

_____

_____

How I'd like to feel before bed

_____

_____

Questions for my Angels before bed

_____

_____

_____

Day _____ **Date** _____

How would I like to feel today? (choose 3)

_____

_____

My intention for the next 3 months

_____

_____

_____

_____

My daily intention

_____

_____

I AM (3-5)

_____

_____

Affirmations or Mantras

_____

_____

_____

1-3 action steps I can take today to co-create my intentions!

_____

_____

_____

_____

_____

Today's Permission Slip

_____

_____

Evening!

3-5 Appreciations from today and why

_____

_____

_____

3 Qualities I Love and value about myself

_____

_____

_____

How I'd like to feel before bed

_____

_____

Questions for my Angels before bed

_____

_____

_____

Day _____ **Date** _____

How would I like to feel today? (choose 3)

_____

_____

My intention for the next 3 months

_____

_____

_____

_____

My daily intention

_____

_____

I AM (3-5)

_____

_____

Affirmations or Mantras

_____

_____

_____

1-3 action steps I can take today to co-create my intentions!

_____

_____

_____

_____

_____

Today's Permission Slip

_____

_____

Evening!

3-5 Appreciations from today and why

_____

_____

_____

3 Qualities I Love and value about myself

_____

_____

_____

How I'd like to feel before bed

_____

_____

Questions for my Angels before bed

_____

_____

_____

Day _____ **Date** _____

How would I like to feel today? (choose 3)

_____

_____

My intention for the next 3 months

_____

_____

_____

_____

My daily intention

_____

_____

I AM (3-5)

_____

_____

Affirmations or Mantras

_____

_____

_____

1-3 action steps I can take today to co-create my intentions!

_____

_____

_____

_____

_____

Today's Permission Slip

_____

_____

Evening!

3-5 Appreciations from today and why

_____

_____

_____

3 Qualities I Love and value about myself

_____

_____

_____

How I'd like to feel before bed

_____

_____

Questions for my Angels before bed

_____

_____

_____

Day _____ **Date** _____

How would I like to feel today? (choose 3)

_____

_____

My intention for the next 3 months

_____

_____

_____

_____

My daily intention

_____

_____

I AM (3-5)

_____

_____

Affirmations or Mantras

_____

_____

_____

1-3 action steps I can take today to co-create my intentions!

_____

_____

_____

_____

_____

Today's Permission Slip

_____

_____

Evening!

3-5 Appreciations from today and why

_____

_____

_____

3 Qualities I Love and value about myself

_____

_____

_____

How I'd like to feel before bed

_____

_____

Questions for my Angels before bed

_____

_____

_____

Day _____ **Date** _____

How would I like to feel today? (choose 3)

_____

_____

My intention for the next 3 months

_____

_____

_____

_____

My daily intention

_____

_____

I AM (3-5)

_____

_____

Affirmations or Mantras

_____

_____

_____

1-3 action steps I can take today to co-create my intentions!

_____

_____

_____

_____

Today's Permission Slip

_____

_____

Evening!

3-5 Appreciations from today and why

_____

_____

_____

3 Qualities I Love and value about myself

_____

_____

_____

How I'd like to feel before bed

_____

_____

Questions for my Angels before bed

_____

_____

_____

Day _____ **Date** _____

How would I like to feel today? (choose 3)

_____

_____

My intention for the next 3 months

_____

_____

_____

_____

My daily intention

_____

_____

I AM (3-5)

_____

_____

Affirmations or Mantras

_____

_____

_____

1-3 action steps I can take today to co-create my intentions!

_____

_____

_____

_____

_____

Today's Permission Slip

_____

_____

Evening!

3-5 Appreciations from today and why

_____

_____

_____

3 Qualities I Love and value about myself

_____

_____

_____

How I'd like to feel before bed

_____

_____

Questions for my Angels before bed

_____

_____

_____

Day _____ **Date** _____

How would I like to feel today? (choose 3)

_____

_____

My intention for the next 3 months

_____

_____

_____

_____

My daily intention

_____

_____

I AM (3-5)

_____

_____

Affirmations or Mantras

_____

_____

_____

1-3 action steps I can take today to co-create my intentions!

_____

_____

_____

_____

Today's Permission Slip

_____

_____

Evening!

3-5 Appreciations from today and why

_____

_____

_____

3 Qualities I Love and value about myself

_____

_____

_____

How I'd like to feel before bed

_____

_____

Questions for my Angels before bed

_____

_____

_____

Day _____ **Date** _____

How would I like to feel today? (choose 3)

_____

_____

My intention for the next 3 months

_____

_____

_____

_____

My daily intention

_____

_____

I AM (3-5)

_____

_____

Affirmations or Mantras

_____

_____

_____

1-3 action steps I can take today to co-create my intentions!

_____

_____

_____

_____

_____

Today's Permission Slip

_____

_____

Evening!

3-5 Appreciations from today and why

_____

_____

_____

3 Qualities I Love and value about myself

_____

_____

_____

How I'd like to feel before bed

_____

_____

Questions for my Angels before bed

_____

_____

_____

Day _____ **Date** _____

How would I like to feel today? (choose 3)

_____

_____

My intention for the next 3 months

_____

_____

_____

_____

My daily intention

_____

_____

I AM (3-5)

_____

_____

Affirmations or Mantras

_____

_____

_____

1-3 action steps I can take today to co-create my intentions!

_____

_____

_____

_____

_____

Today's Permission Slip

_____

_____

Evening!

3-5 Appreciations from today and why

_____

_____

_____

3 Qualities I Love and value about myself

_____

_____

_____

How I'd like to feel before bed

_____

_____

Questions for my Angels before bed

_____

_____

_____

Day _____ **Date** _____

How would I like to feel today? (choose 3)

_____

_____

My intention for the next 3 months

_____

_____

_____

_____

My daily intention

_____

_____

I AM (3-5)

_____

_____

Affirmations or Mantras

_____

_____

_____

1-3 action steps I can take today to co-create my intentions!

_____

_____

_____

_____

_____

Today's Permission Slip

_____

_____

Evening!

3-5 Appreciations from today and why

_____

_____

_____

3 Qualities I Love and value about myself

_____

_____

_____

How I'd like to feel before bed

_____

_____

Questions for my Angels before bed

_____

_____

_____

Day _____ **Date** _____

How would I like to feel today? (choose 3)

_____

_____

My intention for the next 3 months

_____

_____

_____

_____

My daily intention

_____

_____

I AM (3-5)

_____

_____

Affirmations or Mantras

_____

_____

_____

1-3 action steps I can take today to co-create my intentions!

_____

_____

_____

_____

_____

Today's Permission Slip

_____

_____

Evening!

3-5 Appreciations from today and why

_____

_____

_____

3 Qualities I Love and value about myself

_____

_____

_____

How I'd like to feel before bed

_____

_____

Questions for my Angels before bed

_____

_____

_____

Day _____ **Date** _____

How would I like to feel today? (choose 3)

_____

_____

My intention for the next 3 months

_____

_____

_____

_____

My daily intention

_____

_____

I AM (3-5)

_____

_____

Affirmations or Mantras

_____

_____

_____

1-3 action steps I can take today to co-create my intentions!

_____

_____

_____

_____

_____

Today's Permission Slip

_____

_____

Evening!

3-5 Appreciations from today and why

_____

_____

_____

3 Qualities I Love and value about myself

_____

_____

_____

How I'd like to feel before bed

_____

_____

Questions for my Angels before bed

_____

_____

_____

Day _____ **Date** _____

How would I like to feel today? (choose 3)

_____

_____

My intention for the next 3 months

_____

_____

_____

_____

My daily intention

_____

_____

I AM (3-5)

_____

_____

Affirmations or Mantras

_____

_____

_____

1-3 action steps I can take today to co-create my intentions!

_____

_____

_____

_____

_____

Today's Permission Slip

_____

_____

Evening!

3-5 Appreciations from today and why

_____

_____

_____

3 Qualities I Love and value about myself

_____

_____

_____

How I'd like to feel before bed

_____

_____

Questions for my Angels before bed

_____

_____

_____

Day _____ **Date** _____

How would I like to feel today? (choose 3)

_____

_____

My intention for the next 3 months

_____

_____

_____

_____

My daily intention

_____

_____

I AM (3-5)

_____

_____

Affirmations or Mantras

_____

_____

_____

1-3 action steps I can take today to co-create my intentions!

_____

_____

_____

_____

Today's Permission Slip

_____

_____

Evening!

3-5 Appreciations from today and why

_____

_____

_____

3 Qualities I Love and value about myself

_____

_____

_____

How I'd like to feel before bed

_____

_____

Questions for my Angels before bed

_____

_____

_____

Day _____ **Date** _____

How would I like to feel today? (choose 3)

_____

_____

My intention for the next 3 months

_____

_____

_____

_____

My daily intention

_____

_____

I AM (3-5)

_____

_____

Affirmations or Mantras

_____

_____

_____

1-3 action steps I can take today to co-create my intentions!

_____

_____

_____

_____

_____

Today's Permission Slip

_____

_____

Evening!

3-5 Appreciations from today and why

_____

_____

_____

3 Qualities I Love and value about myself

_____

_____

_____

How I'd like to feel before bed

_____

_____

Questions for my Angels before bed

_____

_____

_____

Day _____ **Date** _____

How would I like to feel today? (choose 3)

_____

_____

My intention for the next 3 months

_____

_____

_____

_____

My daily intention

_____

_____

I AM (3-5)

_____

_____

Affirmations or Mantras

_____

_____

_____

1-3 action steps I can take today to co-create my intentions!

_____

_____

_____

_____

_____

Today's Permission Slip

_____

_____

Evening!

3-5 Appreciations from today and why

_____

_____

_____

3 Qualities I Love and value about myself

_____

_____

_____

How I'd like to feel before bed

_____

_____

Questions for my Angels before bed

_____

_____

_____

Day _____ **Date** _____

How would I like to feel today? (choose 3)

_____

_____

My intention for the next 3 months

_____

_____

_____

_____

My daily intention

_____

_____

I AM (3-5)

_____

_____

Affirmations or Mantras

_____

_____

_____

1-3 action steps I can take today to co-create my intentions!

_____

_____

_____

_____

_____

Today's Permission Slip

_____

_____

Evening!

3-5 Appreciations from today and why

_____

_____

_____

3 Qualities I Love and value about myself

_____

_____

_____

How I'd like to feel before bed

_____

_____

Questions for my Angels before bed

_____

_____

_____

Day _____ **Date** _____

How would I like to feel today? (choose 3)

_____

_____

My intention for the next 3 months

_____

_____

_____

_____

My daily intention

_____

_____

I AM (3-5)

_____

_____

Affirmations or Mantras

_____

_____

_____

1-3 action steps I can take today to co-create my intentions!

_____

_____

_____

_____

_____

Today's Permission Slip

_____

_____

Evening!

3-5 Appreciations from today and why

_____

_____

_____

3 Qualities I Love and value about myself

_____

_____

_____

How I'd like to feel before bed

_____

_____

Questions for my Angels before bed

_____

_____

_____

Day _____ **Date** _____

How would I like to feel today? (choose 3)

_____

_____

My intention for the next 3 months

_____

_____

_____

_____

My daily intention

_____

_____

I AM (3-5)

_____

_____

Affirmations or Mantras

_____

_____

_____

1-3 action steps I can take today to co-create my intentions!

_____

_____

_____

_____

_____

Today's Permission Slip

_____

_____

Evening!

3-5 Appreciations from today and why

_____

_____

_____

3 Qualities I Love and value about myself

_____

_____

_____

How I'd like to feel before bed

_____

_____

Questions for my Angels before bed

_____

_____

_____

Day _____ **Date** _____

How would I like to feel today? (choose 3)

_____

_____

My intention for the next 3 months

_____

_____

_____

My daily intention

_____

_____

I AM (3-5)

_____

_____

Affirmations or Mantras

_____

_____

1-3 action steps I can take today to co-create my intentions!

_____

_____

_____

_____

_____

Today's Permission Slip

_____

_____

Evening!

3-5 Appreciations from today and why

_____

_____

_____

3 Qualities I Love and value about myself

_____

_____

_____

How I'd like to feel before bed

_____

_____

Questions for my Angels before bed

_____

_____

_____

Day _____ **Date** _____

How would I like to feel today? (choose 3)

_____

_____

My intention for the next 3 months

_____

_____

_____

_____

My daily intention

_____

_____

I AM (3-5)

_____

_____

Affirmations or Mantras

_____

_____

_____

1-3 action steps I can take today to co-create my intentions!

_____

_____

_____

_____

_____

Today's Permission Slip

_____

_____

Evening!

3-5 Appreciations from today and why

_____

_____

_____

3 Qualities I Love and value about myself

_____

_____

_____

How I'd like to feel before bed

_____

_____

Questions for my Angels before bed

_____

_____

_____

Day _____ **Date** _____

How would I like to feel today? (choose 3)

_____

_____

My intention for the next 3 months

_____

_____

_____

_____

My daily intention

_____

_____

I AM (3-5)

_____

_____

Affirmations or Mantras

_____

_____

_____

1-3 action steps I can take today to co-create my intentions!

_____

_____

_____

_____

_____

Today's Permission Slip

_____

_____

Evening!

3-5 Appreciations from today and why

_____

_____

_____

3 Qualities I Love and value about myself

_____

_____

_____

How I'd like to feel before bed

_____

_____

Questions for my Angels before bed

_____

_____

_____

Day _____ **Date** _____

How would I like to feel today? (choose 3)

_____

_____

My intention for the next 3 months

_____

_____

_____

My daily intention

_____

_____

I AM (3-5)

_____

_____

Affirmations or Mantras

_____

_____

1-3 action steps I can take today to co-create my intentions!

_____

_____

_____

_____

_____

Today's Permission Slip

_____

_____

Evening!

3-5 Appreciations from today and why

_____

_____

_____

3 Qualities I Love and value about myself

_____

_____

_____

How I'd like to feel before bed

_____

_____

Questions for my Angels before bed

_____

_____

_____

Day _____ **Date** _____

How would I like to feel today? (choose 3)

_____

_____

My intention for the next 3 months

_____

_____

_____

My daily intention

_____

_____

I AM (3-5)

_____

_____

Affirmations or Mantras

_____

_____

1-3 action steps I can take today to co-create my intentions!

_____

_____

_____

_____

_____

Today's Permission Slip

_____

_____

Evening!

3-5 Appreciations from today and why

_____

_____

_____

3 Qualities I Love and value about myself

_____

_____

_____

How I'd like to feel before bed

_____

_____

Questions for my Angels before bed

_____

_____

_____

Day _____ **Date** _____

How would I like to feel today? (choose 3)

_____

_____

My intention for the next 3 months

_____

_____

_____

_____

My daily intention

_____

_____

I AM (3-5)

_____

_____

Affirmations or Mantras

_____

_____

_____

1-3 action steps I can take today to co-create my intentions!

_____

_____

_____

_____

_____

Today's Permission Slip

_____

_____

Evening!

3-5 Appreciations from today and why

_____

_____

_____

3 Qualities I Love and value about myself

_____

_____

_____

How I'd like to feel before bed

_____

_____

Questions for my Angels before bed

_____

_____

_____

Day _____ **Date** _____

How would I like to feel today? (choose 3)

_____

_____

My intention for the next 3 months

_____

_____

_____

_____

My daily intention

_____

_____

I AM (3-5)

_____

_____

Affirmations or Mantras

_____

_____

_____

1-3 action steps I can take today to co-create my intentions!

_____

_____

_____

_____

_____

Today's Permission Slip

_____

_____

Evening!

3-5 Appreciations from today and why

_____

_____

_____

3 Qualities I Love and value about myself

_____

_____

_____

How I'd like to feel before bed

_____

_____

Questions for my Angels before bed

_____

_____

_____

Day _____ **Date** _____

How would I like to feel today? (choose 3)

_____

_____

My intention for the next 3 months

_____

_____

_____

_____

My daily intention

_____

_____

I AM (3-5)

_____

_____

Affirmations or Mantras

_____

_____

_____

1-3 action steps I can take today to co-create my intentions!

_____

_____

_____

_____

_____

Today's Permission Slip

_____

_____

Evening!

3-5 Appreciations from today and why

_____

_____

_____

3 Qualities I Love and value about myself

_____

_____

_____

How I'd like to feel before bed

_____

_____

Questions for my Angels before bed

_____

_____

_____

Coloring Page by
JoHenna Design LLC ©
JoHennaDesign.com
Indianapolis, IN

Monthly

Check-In!

Month _____ **Year** _____

Personal Year _____ **Personal Month** _____

You'll write down all your desired feelings...

_____

_____

_____

Next you'll write down your intentions in the areas you're focusing on...

_____

_____

_____

_____

_____

Who I get to be to manifest these intentions

_____

_____

_____

What's not working & why?

_____

_____

_____

What's working & why?

_____

_____

_____

Are my actions in alignment with my values?

My values:

_____

_____

Life Areas

Inner-Divine-Self & Spirituality

Romantic Relationships

Family & Society

Health & Wellness

Lifestyle

Career & Passion!

Financial

Creativity, Learning, Growth

Co-Create

Daily Focus

Day _____ **Date** _____

How would I like to feel today? (choose 3)

_____

_____

My intention for the next 3 months

_____

_____

_____

My daily intention

_____

_____

I AM (3-5)

_____

_____

Affirmations or Mantras

_____

_____

_____

1-3 action steps I can take today to co-create my intentions!

_____

_____

_____

_____

_____

Today's Permission Slip

_____

_____

Evening!

3-5 Appreciations from today and why

_____

_____

_____

3 Qualities I Love and value about myself

_____

_____

_____

How I'd like to feel before bed

_____

_____

Questions for my Angels before bed

_____

_____

_____

Day _____ **Date** _____

How would I like to feel today? (choose 3)

_____

_____

My intention for the next 3 months

_____

_____

_____

_____

My daily intention

_____

_____

I AM (3-5)

_____

_____

Affirmations or Mantras

_____

_____

_____

1-3 action steps I can take today to co-create my intentions!

_____

_____

_____

_____

_____

Today's Permission Slip

_____

_____

Evening!

3-5 Appreciations from today and why

_____

_____

_____

3 Qualities I Love and value about myself

_____

_____

_____

How I'd like to feel before bed

_____

_____

Questions for my Angels before bed

_____

_____

_____

Day _____ **Date** _____

How would I like to feel today? (choose 3)

_____

_____

My intention for the next 3 months

_____

_____

_____

_____

My daily intention

_____

_____

I AM (3-5)

_____

_____

Affirmations or Mantras

_____

_____

_____

1-3 action steps I can take today to co-create my intentions!

_____

_____

_____

_____

_____

Today's Permission Slip

_____

_____

Evening!

3-5 Appreciations from today and why

_____

_____

_____

3 Qualities I Love and value about myself

_____

_____

_____

How I'd like to feel before bed

_____

_____

Questions for my Angels before bed

_____

_____

_____

Day _____ **Date** _____

How would I like to feel today? (choose 3)

_____

_____

My intention for the next 3 months

_____

_____

_____

_____

My daily intention

_____

_____

I AM (3-5)

_____

_____

Affirmations or Mantras

_____

_____

_____

1-3 action steps I can take today to co-create my intentions!

_____

_____

_____

_____

_____

Today's Permission Slip

_____

_____

Evening!

3-5 Appreciations from today and why

_____

_____

_____

3 Qualities I Love and value about myself

_____

_____

_____

How I'd like to feel before bed

_____

_____

Questions for my Angels before bed

_____

_____

_____

Day _____ **Date** _____

How would I like to feel today? (choose 3)

_____

_____

My intention for the next 3 months

_____

_____

_____

_____

My daily intention

_____

_____

I AM (3-5)

_____

_____

Affirmations or Mantras

_____

_____

_____

1-3 action steps I can take today to co-create my intentions!

_____

_____

_____

_____

_____

Today's Permission Slip

_____

_____

Evening!

3-5 Appreciations from today and why

_____

_____

_____

3 Qualities I Love and value about myself

_____

_____

_____

How I'd like to feel before bed

_____

_____

Questions for my Angels before bed

_____

_____

_____

Day _____ **Date** _____

How would I like to feel today? (choose 3)

_____

_____

My intention for the next 3 months

_____

_____

_____

_____

My daily intention

_____

_____

I AM (3-5)

_____

_____

Affirmations or Mantras

_____

_____

_____

1-3 action steps I can take today to co-create my intentions!

_____

_____

_____

_____

Today's Permission Slip

_____

_____

Evening!

3-5 Appreciations from today and why

_____

_____

_____

3 Qualities I Love and value about myself

_____

_____

_____

How I'd like to feel before bed

_____

_____

Questions for my Angels before bed

_____

_____

_____

Day _____ **Date** _____

How would I like to feel today? (choose 3)

_____

_____

My intention for the next 3 months

_____

_____

_____

_____

My daily intention

_____

_____

I AM (3-5)

_____

_____

Affirmations or Mantras

_____

_____

_____

1-3 action steps I can take today to co-create my intentions!

_____

_____

_____

_____

_____

Today's Permission Slip

_____

_____

Evening!

3-5 Appreciations from today and why

_____

_____

_____

3 Qualities I Love and value about myself

_____

_____

_____

How I'd like to feel before bed

_____

_____

Questions for my Angels before bed

_____

_____

_____

Day _____ **Date** _____

How would I like to feel today? (choose 3)

_____

_____

My intention for the next 3 months

_____

_____

_____

My daily intention

_____

_____

I AM (3-5)

_____

_____

Affirmations or Mantras

_____

_____

1-3 action steps I can take today to co-create my intentions!

_____

_____

_____

_____

_____

Today's Permission Slip

_____

_____

Evening!

3-5 Appreciations from today and why

_____

_____

_____

3 Qualities I Love and value about myself

_____

_____

_____

How I'd like to feel before bed

_____

_____

Questions for my Angels before bed

_____

_____

_____

Day _____ **Date** _____

How would I like to feel today? (choose 3)

_____

_____

My intention for the next 3 months

_____

_____

_____

_____

My daily intention

_____

_____

I AM (3-5)

_____

_____

Affirmations or Mantras

_____

_____

_____

1-3 action steps I can take today to co-create my intentions!

_____

_____

_____

_____

_____

Today's Permission Slip

_____

_____

Evening!

3-5 Appreciations from today and why

_____

_____

_____

3 Qualities I Love and value about myself

_____

_____

_____

How I'd like to feel before bed

_____

_____

Questions for my Angels before bed

_____

_____

_____

Day _____ **Date** _____

How would I like to feel today? (choose 3)

_____

_____

My intention for the next 3 months

_____

_____

_____

_____

My daily intention

_____

_____

I AM (3-5)

_____

_____

Affirmations or Mantras

_____

_____

_____

1-3 action steps I can take today to co-create my intentions!

_____

_____

_____

_____

_____

Today's Permission Slip

_____

_____

Evening!

3-5 Appreciations from today and why

_____

_____

_____

3 Qualities I Love and value about myself

_____

_____

_____

How I'd like to feel before bed

_____

_____

Questions for my Angels before bed

_____

_____

_____

Day _____ **Date** _____

How would I like to feel today? (choose 3)

_____

_____

My intention for the next 3 months

_____

_____

_____

My daily intention

_____

_____

I AM (3-5)

_____

_____

Affirmations or Mantras

_____

_____

1-3 action steps I can take today to co-create my intentions!

_____

_____

_____

_____

_____

Today's Permission Slip

_____

_____

Evening!

3-5 Appreciations from today and why

_____

_____

_____

3 Qualities I Love and value about myself

_____

_____

_____

How I'd like to feel before bed

_____

_____

Questions for my Angels before bed

_____

_____

_____

Day _____ **Date** _____

How would I like to feel today? (choose 3)

_____

_____

My intention for the next 3 months

_____

_____

_____

_____

My daily intention

_____

_____

I AM (3-5)

_____

_____

Affirmations or Mantras

_____

_____

_____

1-3 action steps I can take today to co-create my intentions!

_____

_____

_____

_____

_____

Today's Permission Slip

_____

_____

Evening!

3-5 Appreciations from today and why

_____

_____

_____

3 Qualities I Love and value about myself

_____

_____

_____

How I'd like to feel before bed

_____

_____

Questions for my Angels before bed

_____

_____

_____

Day _____ **Date** _____

How would I like to feel today? (choose 3)

_____

_____

My intention for the next 3 months

_____

_____

_____

_____

My daily intention

_____

_____

I AM (3-5)

_____

_____

Affirmations or Mantras

_____

_____

_____

1-3 action steps I can take today to co-create my intentions!

_____

_____

_____

_____

_____

Today's Permission Slip

_____

_____

Evening!

3-5 Appreciations from today and why

_____

_____

_____

3 Qualities I Love and value about myself

_____

_____

_____

How I'd like to feel before bed

_____

_____

Questions for my Angels before bed

_____

_____

_____

Day _____ **Date** _____

How would I like to feel today? (choose 3)

_____

_____

My intention for the next 3 months

_____

_____

_____

My daily intention

_____

_____

I AM (3-5)

_____

_____

Affirmations or Mantras

_____

_____

1-3 action steps I can take today to co-create my intentions!

_____

_____

_____

_____

_____

Today's Permission Slip

_____

_____

Evening!

3-5 Appreciations from today and why

_____

_____

_____

3 Qualities I Love and value about myself

_____

_____

_____

How I'd like to feel before bed

_____

_____

Questions for my Angels before bed

_____

_____

_____

Day _____ **Date** _____

How would I like to feel today? (choose 3)

_____

_____

My intention for the next 3 months

_____

_____

_____

My daily intention

_____

_____

I AM (3-5)

_____

_____

Affirmations or Mantras

_____

_____

_____

1-3 action steps I can take today to co-create my intentions!

_____

_____

_____

_____

_____

Today's Permission Slip

_____

_____

Evening!

3-5 Appreciations from today and why

_____

_____

_____

3 Qualities I Love and value about myself

_____

_____

_____

How I'd like to feel before bed

_____

_____

Questions for my Angels before bed

_____

_____

_____

Day _____ **Date** _____

How would I like to feel today? (choose 3)

_____

_____

My intention for the next 3 months

_____

_____

_____

_____

My daily intention

_____

_____

I AM (3-5)

_____

_____

Affirmations or Mantras

_____

_____

_____

1-3 action steps I can take today to co-create my intentions!

_____

_____

_____

_____

_____

Today's Permission Slip

_____

_____

Evening!

3-5 Appreciations from today and why

_____

_____

_____

3 Qualities I Love and value about myself

_____

_____

_____

How I'd like to feel before bed

_____

_____

Questions for my Angels before bed

_____

_____

_____

Day _____ **Date** _____

How would I like to feel today? (choose 3)

_____

_____

My intention for the next 3 months

_____

_____

_____

My daily intention

_____

_____

I AM (3-5)

_____

_____

Affirmations or Mantras

_____

_____

_____

1-3 action steps I can take today to co-create my intentions!

_____

_____

_____

_____

_____

Today's Permission Slip

_____

_____

Evening!

3-5 Appreciations from today and why

_____

_____

_____

3 Qualities I Love and value about myself

_____

_____

_____

How I'd like to feel before bed

_____

_____

Questions for my Angels before bed

_____

_____

_____

Day _____ **Date** _____

How would I like to feel today? (choose 3)

_____

_____

My intention for the next 3 months

_____

_____

_____

_____

My daily intention

_____

_____

I AM (3-5)

_____

_____

Affirmations or Mantras

_____

_____

_____

1-3 action steps I can take today to co-create my intentions!

_____

_____

_____

_____

_____

Today's Permission Slip

_____

_____

Evening!

3-5 Appreciations from today and why

_____

_____

_____

3 Qualities I Love and value about myself

_____

_____

_____

How I'd like to feel before bed

_____

_____

Questions for my Angels before bed

_____

_____

_____

Day _____ **Date** _____

How would I like to feel today? (choose 3)

_____

_____

My intention for the next 3 months

_____

_____

_____

My daily intention

_____

_____

I AM (3-5)

_____

_____

Affirmations or Mantras

_____

_____

_____

1-3 action steps I can take today to co-create my intentions!

_____

_____

_____

_____

_____

Today's Permission Slip

_____

_____

Evening!

3-5 Appreciations from today and why

_____

_____

_____

3 Qualities I Love and value about myself

_____

_____

_____

How I'd like to feel before bed

_____

_____

Questions for my Angels before bed

_____

_____

_____

Day _____ **Date** _____

How would I like to feel today? (choose 3)

_____

_____

My intention for the next 3 months

_____

_____

_____

My daily intention

_____

_____

I AM (3-5)

_____

_____

Affirmations or Mantras

_____

_____

1-3 action steps I can take today to co-create my intentions!

_____

_____

_____

_____

_____

Today's Permission Slip

_____

_____

Evening!

3-5 Appreciations from today and why

_____

_____

_____

3 Qualities I Love and value about myself

_____

_____

_____

How I'd like to feel before bed

_____

_____

Questions for my Angels before bed

_____

_____

_____

Day _____ **Date** _____

How would I like to feel today? (choose 3)

_____

_____

My intention for the next 3 months

_____

_____

_____

My daily intention

_____

_____

I AM (3-5)

_____

_____

Affirmations or Mantras

_____

_____

_____

1-3 action steps I can take today to co-create my intentions!

_____

_____

_____

_____

_____

Today's Permission Slip

_____

_____

Evening!

3-5 Appreciations from today and why

_____

_____

_____

3 Qualities I Love and value about myself

_____

_____

_____

How I'd like to feel before bed

_____

_____

Questions for my Angels before bed

_____

_____

_____

Day _____ **Date** _____

How would I like to feel today? (choose 3)

_____

_____

My intention for the next 3 months

_____

_____

_____

My daily intention

_____

_____

I AM (3-5)

_____

_____

Affirmations or Mantras

_____

_____

_____

1-3 action steps I can take today to co-create my intentions!

_____

_____

_____

_____

_____

Today's Permission Slip

_____

_____

Evening!

3-5 Appreciations from today and why

_____

_____

_____

3 Qualities I Love and value about myself

_____

_____

_____

How I'd like to feel before bed

_____

_____

Questions for my Angels before bed

_____

_____

_____

Day _____ **Date** _____

How would I like to feel today? (choose 3)

_____

_____

My intention for the next 3 months

_____

_____

_____

_____

My daily intention

_____

_____

I AM (3-5)

_____

_____

Affirmations or Mantras

_____

_____

_____

1-3 action steps I can take today to co-create my intentions!

_____

_____

_____

_____

_____

Today's Permission Slip

_____

_____

Evening!

3-5 Appreciations from today and why

_____

_____

_____

3 Qualities I Love and value about myself

_____

_____

_____

How I'd like to feel before bed

_____

_____

Questions for my Angels before bed

_____

_____

_____

Day _____ **Date** _____

How would I like to feel today? (choose 3)

_____

_____

My intention for the next 3 months

_____

_____

_____

_____

My daily intention

_____

_____

I AM (3-5)

_____

_____

Affirmations or Mantras

_____

_____

_____

1-3 action steps I can take today to co-create my intentions!

_____

_____

_____

_____

_____

Today's Permission Slip

_____

_____

Evening!

3-5 Appreciations from today and why

_____

_____

_____

3 Qualities I Love and value about myself

_____

_____

_____

How I'd like to feel before bed

_____

_____

Questions for my Angels before bed

_____

_____

_____

Day _____ **Date** _____

How would I like to feel today? (choose 3)

_____

_____

My intention for the next 3 months

_____

_____

_____

My daily intention

_____

_____

I AM (3-5)

_____

_____

Affirmations or Mantras

_____

_____

_____

1-3 action steps I can take today to co-create my intentions!

_____

_____

_____

_____

_____

Today's Permission Slip

_____

_____

Evening!

3-5 Appreciations from today and why

_____

_____

_____

3 Qualities I Love and value about myself

_____

_____

_____

How I'd like to feel before bed

_____

_____

Questions for my Angels before bed

_____

_____

_____

Day _____ **Date** _____

How would I like to feel today? (choose 3)

_____

_____

My intention for the next 3 months

_____

_____

_____

My daily intention

_____

_____

I AM (3-5)

_____

_____

Affirmations or Mantras

_____

_____

_____

1-3 action steps I can take today to co-create my intentions!

_____

_____

_____

_____

_____

Today's Permission Slip

_____

_____

Evening!

3-5 Appreciations from today and why

_____

_____

_____

3 Qualities I Love and value about myself

_____

_____

_____

How I'd like to feel before bed

_____

_____

Questions for my Angels before bed

_____

_____

_____

Day _____ **Date** _____

How would I like to feel today? (choose 3)

_____

_____

My intention for the next 3 months

_____

_____

_____

_____

My daily intention

_____

_____

I AM (3-5)

_____

_____

Affirmations or Mantras

_____

_____

_____

1-3 action steps I can take today to co-create my intentions!

_____

_____

_____

_____

Today's Permission Slip

_____

_____

Evening!

3-5 Appreciations from today and why

_____

_____

_____

3 Qualities I Love and value about myself

_____

_____

_____

How I'd like to feel before bed

_____

_____

Questions for my Angels before bed

_____

_____

_____

Day _____ **Date** _____

How would I like to feel today? (choose 3)

_____

_____

My intention for the next 3 months

_____

_____

_____

_____

My daily intention

_____

_____

I AM (3-5)

_____

_____

Affirmations or Mantras

_____

_____

_____

1-3 action steps I can take today to co-create my intentions!

_____

_____

_____

_____

_____

Today's Permission Slip

_____

_____

Evening!

3-5 Appreciations from today and why

_____

_____

_____

3 Qualities I Love and value about myself

_____

_____

_____

How I'd like to feel before bed

_____

_____

Questions for my Angels before bed

_____

_____

_____

Day _____ **Date** _____

How would I like to feel today? (choose 3)

_____

_____

My intention for the next 3 months

_____

_____

_____

My daily intention

_____

_____

I AM (3-5)

_____

_____

Affirmations or Mantras

_____

_____

_____

1-3 action steps I can take today to co-create my intentions!

_____

_____

_____

_____

_____

Today's Permission Slip

_____

_____

Evening!

3-5 Appreciations from today and why

_____

_____

_____

3 Qualities I Love and value about myself

_____

_____

_____

How I'd like to feel before bed

_____

_____

Questions for my Angels before bed

_____

_____

_____

Day _____ **Date** _____

How would I like to feel today? (choose 3)

_____

_____

My intention for the next 3 months

_____

_____

_____

My daily intention

_____

_____

I AM (3-5)

_____

_____

Affirmations or Mantras

_____

_____

1-3 action steps I can take today to co-create my intentions!

_____

_____

_____

_____

_____

Today's Permission Slip

_____

_____

Evening!

3-5 Appreciations from today and why

_____

_____

_____

3 Qualities I Love and value about myself

_____

_____

_____

How I'd like to feel before bed

_____

_____

Questions for my Angels before bed

_____

_____

_____

Day _____ **Date** _____

How would I like to feel today? (choose 3)

_____

_____

My intention for the next 3 months

_____

_____

_____

_____

My daily intention

_____

_____

I AM (3-5)

_____

_____

Affirmations or Mantras

_____

_____

_____

1-3 action steps I can take today to co-create my intentions!

_____

_____

_____

_____

_____

Today's Permission Slip

_____

_____

Evening!

3-5 Appreciations from today and why

_____

_____

_____

3 Qualities I Love and value about myself

_____

_____

_____

How I'd like to feel before bed

_____

_____

Questions for my Angels before bed

_____

_____

_____

Coloring Page by
JoHenna Design LLC ©
JoHennaDesign.com
Indianapolis, IN

Monthly

Check-In!

Month _____ **Year** _____

Personal Year _____ **Personal Month** _____

You'll write down all your desired feelings...

_____

_____

_____

Next you'll write down your intentions in the areas you're focusing on...

_____

_____

_____

_____

_____

Who I get to be to manifest these intentions

_____

_____

_____

What's not working & why?

_____

_____

_____

What's working & why?

_____

_____

_____

Are my actions in alignment with my values?

My values:

_____

_____

Life Areas

Inner-Divine-Self & Spirituality

Romantic Relationships

Family & Society

Health & Wellness

Lifestyle

Career & Passion!

Financial

Creativity, Learning, Growth

Co-Create

Daily Focus

Day _____ **Date** _____

How would I like to feel today? (choose 3)

_____

_____

My intention for the next 3 months

_____

_____

_____

_____

My daily intention

_____

_____

I AM (3-5)

_____

_____

Affirmations or Mantras

_____

_____

_____

1-3 action steps I can take today to co-create my intentions!

_____

_____

_____

_____

_____

Today's Permission Slip

_____

_____

Evening!

3-5 Appreciations from today and why

_____

_____

_____

3 Qualities I Love and value about myself

_____

_____

_____

How I'd like to feel before bed

_____

_____

Questions for my Angels before bed

_____

_____

_____

Day _____ **Date** _____

How would I like to feel today? (choose 3)

_____

_____

My intention for the next 3 months

_____

_____

_____

_____

My daily intention

_____

_____

I AM (3-5)

_____

_____

Affirmations or Mantras

_____

_____

_____

1-3 action steps I can take today to co-create my intentions!

_____

_____

_____

_____

_____

Today's Permission Slip

_____

_____

Evening!

3-5 Appreciations from today and why

_____

_____

_____

3 Qualities I Love and value about myself

_____

_____

_____

How I'd like to feel before bed

_____

_____

Questions for my Angels before bed

_____

_____

_____

Day _____ **Date** _____

How would I like to feel today? (choose 3)

_____

_____

My intention for the next 3 months

_____

_____

_____

_____

My daily intention

_____

_____

I AM (3-5)

_____

_____

Affirmations or Mantras

_____

_____

_____

1-3 action steps I can take today to co-create my intentions!

_____

_____

_____

_____

_____

Today's Permission Slip

_____

_____

Evening!

3-5 Appreciations from today and why

_____

_____

_____

3 Qualities I Love and value about myself

_____

_____

_____

How I'd like to feel before bed

_____

_____

Questions for my Angels before bed

_____

_____

_____

Day _____ **Date** _____

How would I like to feel today? (choose 3)

_____

_____

My intention for the next 3 months

_____

_____

_____

My daily intention

_____

_____

I AM (3-5)

_____

_____

Affirmations or Mantras

_____

_____

_____

1-3 action steps I can take today to co-create my intentions!

_____

_____

_____

_____

_____

Today's Permission Slip

_____

_____

Evening!

3-5 Appreciations from today and why

_____

_____

_____

3 Qualities I Love and value about myself

_____

_____

_____

How I'd like to feel before bed

_____

_____

Questions for my Angels before bed

_____

_____

_____

Day _____ **Date** _____

How would I like to feel today? (choose 3)

_____

_____

My intention for the next 3 months

_____

_____

_____

_____

My daily intention

_____

_____

I AM (3-5)

_____

_____

Affirmations or Mantras

_____

_____

_____

1-3 action steps I can take today to co-create my intentions!

_____

_____

_____

_____

_____

Today's Permission Slip

_____

_____

Evening!

3-5 Appreciations from today and why

_____

_____

_____

3 Qualities I Love and value about myself

_____

_____

_____

How I'd like to feel before bed

_____

_____

Questions for my Angels before bed

_____

_____

_____

Day _____ **Date** _____

How would I like to feel today? (choose 3)

_____

_____

My intention for the next 3 months

_____

_____

_____

_____

My daily intention

_____

_____

I AM (3-5)

_____

_____

Affirmations or Mantras

_____

_____

1-3 action steps I can take today to co-create my intentions!

_____

_____

_____

_____

_____

Today's Permission Slip

_____

_____

Evening!

3-5 Appreciations from today and why

_____

_____

_____

3 Qualities I Love and value about myself

_____

_____

_____

How I'd like to feel before bed

_____

_____

Questions for my Angels before bed

_____

_____

_____

Day _____ **Date** _____

How would I like to feel today? (choose 3)

_____

_____

My intention for the next 3 months

_____

_____

_____

My daily intention

_____

_____

I AM (3-5)

_____

_____

Affirmations or Mantras

_____

_____

1-3 action steps I can take today to co-create my intentions!

_____

_____

_____

_____

_____

Today's Permission Slip

_____

_____

Evening!

3-5 Appreciations from today and why

_____

_____

_____

3 Qualities I Love and value about myself

_____

_____

_____

How I'd like to feel before bed

_____

_____

Questions for my Angels before bed

_____

_____

Day _____ **Date** _____

How would I like to feel today? (choose 3)

_____

_____

My intention for the next 3 months

_____

_____

_____

_____

My daily intention

_____

_____

I AM (3-5)

_____

_____

Affirmations or Mantras

_____

_____

_____

1-3 action steps I can take today to co-create my intentions!

_____

_____

_____

_____

_____

Today's Permission Slip

_____

_____

Evening!

3-5 Appreciations from today and why

_____

_____

_____

3 Qualities I Love and value about myself

_____

_____

_____

How I'd like to feel before bed

_____

_____

Questions for my Angels before bed

_____

_____

_____

Day _____ **Date** _____

How would I like to feel today? (choose 3)

_____

_____

My intention for the next 3 months

_____

_____

_____

My daily intention

_____

_____

I AM (3-5)

_____

_____

Affirmations or Mantras

_____

_____

1-3 action steps I can take today to co-create my intentions!

_____

_____

_____

_____

Today's Permission Slip

_____

_____

Evening!

3-5 Appreciations from today and why

_____

_____

_____

3 Qualities I Love and value about myself

_____

_____

_____

How I'd like to feel before bed

_____

_____

Questions for my Angels before bed

_____

_____

_____

Day _____ **Date** _____

How would I like to feel today? (choose 3)

_____

_____

My intention for the next 3 months

_____

_____

_____

My daily intention

_____

_____

I AM (3-5)

_____

_____

Affirmations or Mantras

_____

_____

_____

1-3 action steps I can take today to co-create my intentions!

_____

_____

_____

_____

Today's Permission Slip

_____

_____

Evening!

3-5 Appreciations from today and why

_____

_____

_____

3 Qualities I Love and value about myself

_____

_____

_____

How I'd like to feel before bed

_____

_____

Questions for my Angels before bed

_____

_____

_____

Day _____ **Date** _____

How would I like to feel today? (choose 3)

_____

_____

My intention for the next 3 months

_____

_____

_____

My daily intention

_____

_____

I AM (3-5)

_____

_____

Affirmations or Mantras

_____

_____

_____

1-3 action steps I can take today to co-create my intentions!

_____

_____

_____

_____

_____

Today's Permission Slip

_____

_____

Evening!

3-5 Appreciations from today and why

_____

_____

_____

3 Qualities I Love and value about myself

_____

_____

_____

How I'd like to feel before bed

_____

_____

Questions for my Angels before bed

_____

_____

_____

Day _____ **Date** _____

How would I like to feel today? (choose 3)

_____

_____

My intention for the next 3 months

_____

_____

_____

_____

My daily intention

_____

_____

I AM (3-5)

_____

_____

Affirmations or Mantras

_____

_____

_____

1-3 action steps I can take today to co-create my intentions!

_____

_____

_____

_____

_____

Today's Permission Slip

_____

_____

Evening!

3-5 Appreciations from today and why

_____

_____

_____

3 Qualities I Love and value about myself

_____

_____

_____

How I'd like to feel before bed

_____

_____

Questions for my Angels before bed

_____

_____

_____

Day _____ **Date** _____

How would I like to feel today? (choose 3)

_____

_____

My intention for the next 3 months

_____

_____

_____

_____

My daily intention

_____

_____

I AM (3-5)

_____

_____

Affirmations or Mantras

_____

_____

_____

1-3 action steps I can take today to co-create my intentions!

_____

_____

_____

_____

_____

Today's Permission Slip

_____

_____

Evening!

3-5 Appreciations from today and why

_____

_____

_____

3 Qualities I Love and value about myself

_____

_____

_____

How I'd like to feel before bed

_____

_____

Questions for my Angels before bed

_____

_____

_____

Day _____ **Date** _____

How would I like to feel today? (choose 3)

_____

_____

My intention for the next 3 months

_____

_____

_____

My daily intention

_____

_____

I AM (3-5)

_____

_____

Affirmations or Mantras

_____

_____

_____

1-3 action steps I can take today to co-create my intentions!

_____

_____

_____

_____

_____

Today's Permission Slip

_____

_____

Evening!

3-5 Appreciations from today and why

_____

_____

_____

3 Qualities I Love and value about myself

_____

_____

_____

How I'd like to feel before bed

_____

_____

Questions for my Angels before bed

_____

_____

Day _____ **Date** _____

How would I like to feel today? (choose 3)

_____

_____

My intention for the next 3 months

_____

_____

_____

My daily intention

_____

_____

I AM (3-5)

_____

_____

Affirmations or Mantras

_____

_____

1-3 action steps I can take today to co-create my intentions!

_____

_____

_____

_____

_____

Today's Permission Slip

_____

_____

Evening!

3-5 Appreciations from today and why

_____

_____

_____

3 Qualities I Love and value about myself

_____

_____

_____

How I'd like to feel before bed

_____

_____

Questions for my Angels before bed

_____

_____

_____

Day _____ **Date** _____

How would I like to feel today? (choose 3)

_____

_____

My intention for the next 3 months

_____

_____

_____

My daily intention

_____

_____

I AM (3-5)

_____

_____

Affirmations or Mantras

_____

_____

1-3 action steps I can take today to co-create my intentions!

_____

_____

_____

_____

_____

Today's Permission Slip

_____

_____

Evening!

3-5 Appreciations from today and why

_____

_____

_____

3 Qualities I Love and value about myself

_____

_____

_____

How I'd like to feel before bed

_____

_____

Questions for my Angels before bed

_____

_____

_____

Day _____ **Date** _____

How would I like to feel today? (choose 3)

_____

_____

My intention for the next 3 months

_____

_____

_____

My daily intention

_____

_____

I AM (3-5)

_____

_____

Affirmations or Mantras

_____

_____

_____

1-3 action steps I can take today to co-create my intentions!

_____

_____

_____

_____

_____

Today's Permission Slip

_____

_____

Evening!

3-5 Appreciations from today and why

_____

_____

_____

3 Qualities I Love and value about myself

_____

_____

_____

How I'd like to feel before bed

_____

_____

Questions for my Angels before bed

_____

_____

_____

Day _____ **Date** _____

How would I like to feel today? (choose 3)

_____

_____

My intention for the next 3 months

_____

_____

_____

_____

My daily intention

_____

_____

I AM (3-5)

_____

_____

Affirmations or Mantras

_____

_____

_____

1-3 action steps I can take today to co-create my intentions!

_____

_____

_____

_____

_____

Today's Permission Slip

_____

_____

Evening!

3-5 Appreciations from today and why

_____

_____

_____

3 Qualities I Love and value about myself

_____

_____

_____

How I'd like to feel before bed

_____

_____

Questions for my Angels before bed

_____

_____

_____

Day _____ **Date** _____

How would I like to feel today? (choose 3)

_____

_____

My intention for the next 3 months

_____

_____

_____

My daily intention

_____

_____

I AM (3-5)

_____

_____

Affirmations or Mantras

_____

_____

_____

1-3 action steps I can take today to co-create my intentions!

_____

_____

_____

_____

_____

Today's Permission Slip

_____

_____

Evening!

3-5 Appreciations from today and why

_____

_____

_____

3 Qualities I Love and value about myself

_____

_____

_____

How I'd like to feel before bed

_____

_____

Questions for my Angels before bed

_____

_____

_____

Day _____ **Date** _____

How would I like to feel today? (choose 3)

_____

_____

My intention for the next 3 months

_____

_____

_____

My daily intention

_____

_____

I AM (3-5)

_____

_____

Affirmations or Mantras

_____

_____

_____

1-3 action steps I can take today to co-create my intentions!

_____

_____

_____

_____

_____

Today's Permission Slip

_____

_____

Evening!

3-5 Appreciations from today and why

_____

_____

_____

3 Qualities I Love and value about myself

_____

_____

_____

How I'd like to feel before bed

_____

_____

Questions for my Angels before bed

_____

_____

_____

Day _____ **Date** _____

How would I like to feel today? (choose 3)

_____

_____

My intention for the next 3 months

_____

_____

_____

My daily intention

_____

_____

I AM (3-5)

_____

_____

Affirmations or Mantras

_____

_____

1-3 action steps I can take today to co-create my intentions!

_____

_____

_____

_____

_____

Today's Permission Slip

_____

_____

Evening!

3-5 Appreciations from today and why

_____

_____

_____

3 Qualities I Love and value about myself

_____

_____

_____

How I'd like to feel before bed

_____

_____

Questions for my Angels before bed

_____

_____

_____

Day _____ **Date** _____

Angel Card & meaning for today!

_____

_____

How would I like to feel today? (choose 3)

_____

_____

My intention for the next 3 months

_____

_____

My daily intention

_____

_____

I AM (3-5)

_____

_____

Affirmations or Mantras

_____

_____

1-3 action steps I can take today to co-create my intentions!

_____

_____

_____

_____

_____

Today's Permission Slip

_____

_____

Evening!

3-5 Appreciations from today and why

_____

_____

_____

3 Qualities I Love and value about myself

_____

_____

_____

How I'd like to feel before bed

_____

_____

Questions for my Angels before bed

_____

_____

_____

Day _____ **Date** _____

How would I like to feel today? (choose 3)

_____

_____

My intention for the next 3 months

_____

_____

_____

My daily intention

_____

_____

I AM (3-5)

_____

_____

Affirmations or Mantras

_____

_____

1-3 action steps I can take today to co-create my intentions!

_____

_____

_____

_____

_____

Today's Permission Slip

_____

_____

Evening!

3-5 Appreciations from today and why

_____

_____

_____

3 Qualities I Love and value about myself

_____

_____

_____

How I'd like to feel before bed

_____

_____

Questions for my Angels before bed

_____

_____

_____

Day _____ **Date** _____

How would I like to feel today? (choose 3)

_____

_____

My intention for the next 3 months

_____

_____

_____

My daily intention

_____

_____

I AM (3-5)

_____

_____

Affirmations or Mantras

_____

_____

1-3 action steps I can take today to co-create my intentions!

_____

_____

_____

_____

Today's Permission Slip

_____

_____

Evening!

3-5 Appreciations from today and why

_____

_____

_____

3 Qualities I Love and value about myself

_____

_____

_____

How I'd like to feel before bed

_____

_____

Questions for my Angels before bed

_____

_____

Day _____ **Date** _____

How would I like to feel today? (choose 3)

_____

_____

My intention for the next 3 months

_____

_____

_____

_____

My daily intention

_____

_____

I AM (3-5)

_____

_____

Affirmations or Mantras

_____

_____

_____

1-3 action steps I can take today to co-create my intentions!

_____

_____

_____

_____

_____

Today's Permission Slip

_____

_____

Evening!

3-5 Appreciations from today and why

_____

_____

_____

3 Qualities I Love and value about myself

_____

_____

_____

How I'd like to feel before bed

_____

_____

Questions for my Angels before bed

_____

_____

_____

Day _____ **Date** _____

How would I like to feel today? (choose 3)

_____

_____

My intention for the next 3 months

_____

_____

_____

_____

My daily intention

_____

_____

I AM (3-5)

_____

_____

Affirmations or Mantras

_____

_____

_____

1-3 action steps I can take today to co-create my intentions!

_____

_____

_____

_____

_____

Today's Permission Slip

_____

_____

Evening!

3-5 Appreciations from today and why

_____

_____

_____

3 Qualities I Love and value about myself

_____

_____

_____

How I'd like to feel before bed

_____

_____

Questions for my Angels before bed

_____

_____

Day _____ **Date** _____

How would I like to feel today? (choose 3)

_____

_____

My intention for the next 3 months

_____

_____

_____

My daily intention

_____

_____

I AM (3-5)

_____

_____

Affirmations or Mantras

_____

_____

1-3 action steps I can take today to co-create my intentions!

_____

_____

_____

_____

_____

Today's Permission Slip

_____

_____

Evening!

3-5 Appreciations from today and why

_____

_____

_____

3 Qualities I Love and value about myself

_____

_____

_____

How I'd like to feel before bed

_____

_____

Questions for my Angels before bed

_____

_____

_____

Day _____ **Date** _____

How would I like to feel today? (choose 3)

_____

_____

My intention for the next 3 months

_____

_____

_____

My daily intention

_____

_____

I AM (3-5)

_____

_____

Affirmations or Mantras

_____

_____

1-3 action steps I can take today to co-create my intentions!

_____

_____

_____

_____

_____

Today's Permission Slip

_____

_____

Evening!

3-5 Appreciations from today and why

_____

_____

_____

3 Qualities I Love and value about myself

_____

_____

_____

How I'd like to feel before bed

_____

_____

Questions for my Angels before bed

_____

_____

_____

Day _____ **Date** _____

How would I like to feel today? (choose 3)

_____

_____

My intention for the next 3 months

_____

_____

_____

My daily intention

_____

_____

I AM (3-5)

_____

_____

Affirmations or Mantras

_____

_____

_____

1-3 action steps I can take today to co-create my intentions!

_____

_____

_____

_____

_____

Today's Permission Slip

_____

_____

Evening!

3-5 Appreciations from today and why

_____

_____

_____

3 Qualities I Love and value about myself

_____

_____

_____

How I'd like to feel before bed

_____

_____

Questions for my Angels before bed

_____

_____

_____

Day _____ **Date** _____

How would I like to feel today? (choose 3)

_____

_____

My intention for the next 3 months

_____

_____

_____

My daily intention

_____

_____

I AM (3-5)

_____

_____

Affirmations or Mantras

_____

_____

_____

1-3 action steps I can take today to co-create my intentions!

_____

_____

_____

_____

_____

Today's Permission Slip

_____

_____

Evening!

3-5 Appreciations from today and why

_____

_____

_____

3 Qualities I Love and value about myself

_____

_____

_____

How I'd like to feel before bed

_____

_____

Questions for my Angels before bed

_____

_____

_____

Day _____ **Date** _____

How would I like to feel today? (choose 3)

_____

_____

My intention for the next 3 months

_____

_____

_____

My daily intention

_____

_____

I AM (3-5)

_____

_____

Affirmations or Mantras

_____

_____

_____

1-3 action steps I can take today to co-create my intentions!

_____

_____

_____

_____

_____

Today's Permission Slip

_____

_____

Evening!

3-5 Appreciations from today and why

_____

_____

_____

3 Qualities I Love and value about myself

_____

_____

_____

How I'd like to feel before bed

_____

_____

Questions for my Angels before bed

_____

_____

_____

Congratulations on showing up for yourself consistently for
3 months!

Look at how powerful YOU are! You can create anything you'd like
and this is only the beginning.

Are you ready to experience fulfillment, clarity, and joy as you create
a life you Love living - on purpose?! The next step is waiting for you
at www.hearts-joy.com.

Continue showing up, getting curious, and doing your work! This is
a journey and I look forward to walking with you along your journey.

Sending you Much Love!